DECIDE

— TO —

LEAD

LEADERSHIP IS A **CHOICE** **NOT** A TITLE

The Four Questions Anyone Who Wants to Lead Others Must Be Able to Answer

---

by **RUSS HILL**

This book is dedicated to my wife who has made my entire career possible, my kids who have given my life so much additional meaning, and my parents who both taught me how to work hard and convinced me I could do anything I ever dreamed possible.

Table of Contents

Introduction

*h*ave you ever noticed how just one person can completely change the results of an organization or a team?

Think about your experience with most chain restaurants, stores, airlines, or even fitness clubs. One location or crew delivers a terrible customer experience and another one leaves you amazed at how well you were treated. You can't wait to reward one with your loyalty while you swear to never give the other one another dime of your hard-earned money.

Why the difference?

Why do some teams and organizations achieve extraordinary results and others flounder?

My experiences over the last 15 years have convinced me it all comes down to leadership. The leader makes an enormous impact on the performance of a team. I've always known this to be true, but once I began traveling the world and gained access to hundreds of board rooms and internal corporate conferences and meetings, I discovered the performance of a team is entirely determined by its leader.

I'm not the only one reaching this conclusion. On the coming pages, I'll share data that will convince you leaders make or break organizations. You already know this from your own experiences, but the numbers show it as well.

The battle for great leaders is intensifying. The value of leaders who have the skills to align a team to deliver results is soaring in this competitive economy. People with strong leadership skills can basically punch their own ticket. The reality is there aren't enough of them.

I wrote this book for one basic reason: to help create more exceptional leaders. The companies I'm working with desperately need you. This book is one part of my personal plan to reach the broadest audience possible. After flying on more than 600 planes to cities around the world over just the last several years, I have realized I am not making enough of an impact. I need to start writing books and producing a lot more content on a daily basis if I am to fulfill my own purpose of helping create more great leaders.

The Truth About Leadership

Several months ago, I was facilitating a meeting of the top 200 leaders of a large healthcare company. Our firm was brought in after the annual employee engagement survey landed like a 1200-pound bomb. After a few months of helping the top leaders start to identify what needed to shift in their culture, we found ourselves in a large ballroom with the senior executives and expanded leadership team. We put flipcharts around the spacious meeting hall with the titles of different teams and divisions on each one. Then, we asked the people in the room to rotate from flipchart to flipchart and write appreciative and constructive feedback about each team on their flipchart.

After allowing time for each team to weigh in on each flipchart, we sent the groups back to the large sheet of paper that contained the feedback for their team. Each team then read through the comments and then reported out on their observations and plan moving forward.

The meeting ended with the CEO of 18,000 employees reporting out on the feedback his executive team had received from the hundreds of people in the room. Standing in the front of the ballroom and holding a microphone he said, "I've come to realize an inconvenient and disgusting truth. I am the problem."

It was a game-changing moment in the organization. That seasoned and smart executive had seemingly lost touch with just how significant an impact a leader has on a team. Most leaders look at the metrics and rattle off what everyone *else* needs to do to improve or grow performance. They spend too little time considering how their leadership is impacting the team and its performance.

This book is based on observing leaders in hundreds of organizations, studying internal employee engagement data across many industries, interviewing and coaching senior executives and mid-level managers, and determining what specific things leaders do that move the needle in significant ways.

This book isn't about me. Yet because most of you have never met me, I should provide a little more context about whose voice you're hearing as you read these pages. During any given week, I might be in London, Singapore, Sydney, New York, or Kansas City. I wrote this book not as someone who has mastered the art of leading others but rather as someone who is in the trenches with people like you working to deliver results.

The leaders I work with run national restaurant chains, global retail companies, automotive manufacturers, health insurance companies, hospitals, energy companies, food product plants, defense contractors, and everything in between. Some of these leaders have tens of thousands of people who ultimately report up through them. Others manage teams of two to three people.

I've seen the best of the best. I've also encountered the worst of the worst.

My Personal Leadership Journey

Before I helped lead our consulting firm, I led teams in the media business. You'll read about some of my experiences as a broadcast news and sports executive. I've also spent years leading thousands of people in my church. Leading people in a religious organization has meant helping individuals overcome destructive addictions, heal relationships, and make hard decisions that impact their entire lives. I've been responsible for leading teams seeking higher ratings in the media business and I've been responsible for helping people fight a drug addiction that is literally threatening their survival.

I'm also a dad. I care deeply about the four kids I've spent the last 17 years trying to lead alongside my wife.

I've made just about every mistake a leader can make in the corporate world, at church, and in our home. These pages contain not only what I've learned observing other leaders, but the things I've learned in trying to be an effective one myself.

No matter where you are on the leadership spectrum – completely inexperienced or a veteran of managing large global teams – I wrote this book to help you improve your leadership skills. The leadership ability of an individual isn't something that is fixed and permanent. It gets stronger as we learn new things, consider different approaches and methods, and hear what's worked or backfired for others.

Leadership isn't about the genes you were born with or how you were raised. Yes, these factors can impact whether you're naturally gifted with a few leadership traits, but they're far from enough. Becoming a great leader is hard work. It's a painful process that requires intention, determination, confidence, and a willingness to expose vulnerability. This book will help you strengthen your leadership skills. It will build on some ideas and thoughts you already have and it will present some new ways of thinking about how to lead others.

Can I Ask You Four Questions?

I've structured this book around four questions. Each chapter is centered on one of them. The questions are the four most important questions, in my mind, that should be considered by anyone who has a desire to be a great leader. I've spent a significant amount of time considering what these questions should be. My decision was based on the qualities I have seen in leaders whose teams achieve and sustain extraordinary results or who positively impact a significant amount of lives.

As you read each chapter, I invite you to carefully consider the central question posed in it and honestly reflect on your strengths and weaknesses. I encourage you to ask those who know you best for feedback on how they would answer the questions about you. The questions are designed to provoke thought and improvement in the young and inexperienced as well as the seasoned and senior executive.

I purposefully limited the length and depth of this book. I want it to be a quick read that feels more like a personal interview than a wordy formal dissertation. I want you to picture the two of us sitting in a local café having a conversation over lunch. What follows are some of the questions I'd ask you if I had that opportunity. I hope you'll spend some time considering your responses and making any adjustments you deem appropriate in how you lead others or run your department or organization.

An Invitation to Join the Conversation

The final request I have before we dive in is that you go to decidetoleadbook.com and join the conversation with other people reading this book. There are additional tools I've made available there to maximize the impact of reading this book, including documents you can print off and use while reading each chapter as well as a mini online course that takes each of these topics and helps you incorporate them into your life so you can immediately see results in your career and personal life.

I didn't just write this book to give you a few interesting ideas to consider. I wrote it to broaden the impact you can have in the lives of others and to advance your career. The steps outlined here have transformed organizations and propelled leaders to new levels of success. These ideas and steps aren't ones I made up. They're what I've observed over several years of studying and working with leaders in all industries make the difference between people who are stuck and those who are having significant impact.

Some of you have already been to the site and got this book shipped to you from there. I encourage you to participate in the private Facebook group and monthly live chats on Facebook and to complete the course work as you make your way through this book.

All the details about how to join in the conversation and deepen the impact of what you're reading here is at *decidetoleadbook. com*. I've spent months building the learning tools you'll find there. Choose which ones you want to utilize to impact your ability to lead others now and throughout the rest of your life.

**ACTION
ITEMS**

■ Join the conversation by going
to **decidetoleadbook.com**
and utilizing some of the tools
available there to impact your
ability to lead others.

■ Connect with Russ on LinkedIn:
LinkedIn.com/in/russleads for
daily videos and tips

"Leadership is a choice,
not a position."

———

STEPHEN **COVEY**

Decide to Lead

*O*ne Saturday morning when I was a teenager, I decided to grab our family basketball and head out to the rusty basketball hoop my dad had haphazardly attached above the garage door on our modest two-story home.

As I dribbled the ball on our sloped driveway, a car drove up and stopped. The driver exited the car and started walking toward me. He was dressed in slacks, a button-down shirt, and a tie. I recognized him as someone who attended our church and worked for the local NBC TV station. Everyone in our congregation knew he was the guy on the TV news.

To my surprise, he knew my name! He said, "Russell, I've heard you're interested in the news business. Is that true?"

From my earliest days as a child, I had always wanted to be a news reporter.

"Yeah, that's true," I responded.

"What would you think about maybe coming down to the TV station and spending the day with me sometime?" he asked.

I distinctly remember wondering if I was dreaming. *Was this really happening?* Did this man I hadn't even officially met just ask me to go spend a day in a place I've always wanted to work?

Two weeks later, Art Rascon drove up to my driveway again. This time, instead of wearing shorts and a t-shirt, I was in slacks and a button-down shirt. I climbed into his car and spent the day in the NBC newsroom in downtown San Antonio and riding around in a television news truck.

That experience changed me.

A few years later, I began work as a weekend news reporter for a radio station almost no one listened to. I was still in high school and felt like I had launched my path to greatness.

One night after I graduated high school, Art called. By then, he lived in Los Angeles and rioting had broken out after the verdict in the Rodney King trial. Art told me I needed to get on a plane and come to L.A. immediately to cover what was certain to become a huge story that could propel my career in the news business forward.

Within 24 hours, I was in L.A. doing my first television live news report.

Art went on to become a correspondent for the CBS Evening News. I spent 16 years in the broadcast news business.

It all started on that driveway when I was holding a basketball. Art Rascon made a decision to drive by my home on the way to work, and offer to mentor a nerdy teenager. At that moment, he became someone who would have a profound impact on my life. He helped lead me to where I needed to go and encouraged me to do what I needed to do in order to start a successful career in broadcast news.

Leadership Is a Choice

Great leaders often have a major impact on people's lives. They change a person or organization's future. Their influence is like ripples in a body of water. It stretches far and wide, often affecting countless people both directly and indirectly. No one can make you a leader. Sure, they can give you the responsibility to manage a group of people or they can ask you to help someone else. Yes, they can ask others to listen or report to you. But they cannot convince others to follow you.

Leadership is a choice.

Whether or not someone becomes a great leader is first determined by their answer to this simple yet critical question:

QUESTION #1
Do you want to be a leader?

The question is a basic one. It might even seem obvious in a book about leadership. It should not, however, be treated dismissively. The impact of the answer to this question on a person's life is profound. Whether or not someone decides to have children is based, in part, on the answer to that single question. Our answer to this question drives how we respond when we face obstacles that are taller and wider than we anticipated. Our response determines how much influence we will have on the lives of other people. This first question really comes down to probing how much you want to impact others.

Amazon CEO and founder Jeff Bezos was asked in an interview at a business conference in 2018 what it felt like to be the richest man in the world. He said, "I own 16% of Amazon [stock]. Amazon is worth roughly a trillion dollars. That means what we have built over 20 years is $840 billion in wealth for other people. That's what we've done. That's great…and how it should be."

Bezos has created a very nice lifestyle for himself, to say the least, but more importantly, his decision to be a leader has influenced millions of lives – the lives of customers, employees, and shareholders. If I asked you to consider everyone who has had a significant impact on your life, every name you come up with would be someone who made a decision to lead. It might have been a decision they made to lead in a specific moment by doing something that required courage. Or, it could have been their willingness to invest in you by teaching you something, sharing some advice, or sacrificing their time, energy, or substance to positively affect your life.

My friend Tom Smith, one of the co-authors of *The Oz Principle*, likes to say, "Leadership is facilitating movement in the desired direction in a way people feel good about."

The leadership coach and author John C. Maxwell said, "Leadership is not about titles, positions, or flowcharts. It is about one life influencing another."

What 'Leadership' Really Means

We use the word *leader* too casually. We often call people in positions of authority leaders when so many of them are leading us nowhere. Leadership is about getting movement and influencing others. I have been surprised by the number of people in leadership positions I have associated with who have generated hardly any movement or haven't even defined what influence they wish to have on their team or others.

It has been eye-opening to me as I've traveled the world these last several years interacting with tens of thousands of senior executives, directors, and managers just how few of them have had any formal training in leading others. Organizations identify individual contributors who seem committed and elevate them to positions of so-called "leadership" without giving them any help in understanding how to lead people or where, exactly, they're supposed to be leading their teams.

These front-line employees are enticed by the higher pay or prestige that comes with a new title and then quickly find themselves frustrated by the fact that people question them, don't follow their policies and directions, or fail to be as committed as they are to the work.

Organizations elevate people to a leadership team or even the senior leadership team who have no clue what it even means to be a leader.

Every week, I'm in front of managers, speaking to them in groups of 20 to 2,000 individuals, depending on the setting. I regularly get sustained applause from these crowds after offering even the most basic and simplest help in understanding the concept of leadership. We *must* do a better job of developing leaders. I have devoted the last several years of my life to it, and this book is my latest effort.

Leadership Is About Results

Jeff is the CEO of a food manufacturing company. His company's products are found on the shelves of gas stations, grocery stores, Walmart, and Costco. They have plants in the United States and Mexico that employ thousands of people.

By most measures, the company was doing relatively well

when Jeff took over as its leader. He's not the complacent type, however, so Jeff started to think about the potential of the company. He had big dreams. Before any of them could be accomplished, he decided he needed to address one critical measure: employee engagement. The survey results weren't terrible, but they weren't exceptional either.

Jeff decided his leadership team could change this. He elevated employee engagement to one of the three metrics the company would use to determine whether or not it produced a successful year. The other two were top-line revenue and profit.

With great urgency, Jeff and his senior leadership team went to work to lift employee morale. Within eight months, the annual survey results were released and the company's performance had significantly improved. They went from being mediocre to best-in-class. In less than 12 months, thousands of employees were feeling much better about where they worked and how their teams were being led.

Jeff didn't stop there. As he thought about it, he decided a workforce that was more engaged should theoretically be able to produce stronger results. So, he set a goal of a 99% fill rate for orders of frozen burritos, guacamole, salsa, and tortilla chips, among other things that were produced in the company's factories. When Jeff proposed making the fill rate one of the three annual Key Results, he was met with skepticism. A 99% fill rate allows hardly any room for mistakes throughout the year.

Twelve months later, the company celebrated another

successful employee engagement survey and achieved its goal of a 99% fill rate!

When Jeff was made CEO of that company, no one told him he should make the organization a leader in employee engagement or a model of efficiency in food manufacturing. He decided he wanted to lead his team of thousands of employees to achieve things they had never accomplished before. His decision to lead his organization to a place it had not yet been was intentional. He did it after carefully considering what it would require and the possibility that he would not be successful.

Jeff understood that leadership is all about delivering results. At the end of the day, great leaders move the needle. Their impact is measurable. The job is not to run a meeting or produce a schedule. Leaders mobilize people to deliver different results than they are currently achieving. We'll speak more in the coming pages about how great leaders define their desired results and align people around them.

Before we get too much deeper into the tactical part of this book, however, I want to make sure we're all aligned around the impact of answering Question #1 – *Do You Want to Be A Leader* – with a resounding "yes!"

The Pressures of Leading

"I find one thing very motivating – I love people counting on me. And, so, today it's easy to be motivated because we have millions of people counting on me," said Amazon's Bezos. Amazon has millions of customers, investors, and now more than half a million employees.

Many of us would find the pressure of all those people depending on us crushing. Some people find it difficult to have *anyone* counting on them. That's why this book begins with Question #1. Before we can get any deeper into a discussion of what makes someone a great leader, we have to draw a line in the sand. On one side of the line are those who are perfectly comfortable being a follower in all areas of their lives. On the other side of the line are those who have a desire – and a willingness – to lead.

The reality is just because you want to be a leader doesn't make you a great leader. It doesn't even make you a decent leader. The world has no shortage of lame (or said in a nicer way, ineffective) leaders.

When you Decide to Lead, you're walking out from behind the curtain and on to the stage under the bright, hot lights. You're leaving the shadows. You're raising your hand. You're leaving the bench and running on to the court, ready to grab the ball.

Deciding to lead means you are willing to be criticized, questioned, and challenged in front of everyone. It means you are willing to own the failures. Leadership brings with it a magnifying glass that causes people to not only see but often bring attention to your blemishes, contradictions, and weaknesses.

Being a leader looks easy. Almost everyone thinks they can do it. Walk into any organization and just listen to people talk about all the things the leader of their company should be doing. To them, the best course of action seems so obvious. Employees wonder, how could the leader possibly be so clueless?

Being the leader sometimes totally sucks. There are many days when you'll wonder – is this really worth it?

Leadership Is Incredibly Challenging

I've spent my entire life going to church every Sunday. A few years ago, I was asked to serve as the leader of our congregation of more than 500 people. The assignment was temporary – just a few years – and although I was shocked to be asked I thought I had a decent idea of what it would require. After all, I had spent my whole life watching people take turns leading our congregation.

Part of my assignment was managing the charitable funds donated by our members. I was to distribute some of them each month to individuals and families in need. I took this part of my job very seriously. No one wants the money they donate to a church to be wasted.

Late one Sunday, I was in my office at the church. Remember, this was a volunteer assignment – I wasn't paid to do this job that was in addition to my full-time professional job. I was about to meet with a single mom who relied on financial help from the church for years. It had become obvious that she had become overly dependent on these funds, and the assistance was actually damaging her ability to be self-reliant. She couldn't see it, but her reliance on others for more than a temporary period of time had lowered her feelings of self-worth, work ethic, and even her health.

Months before this meeting with this wonderful woman, I had begun working with her to build a budget and a plan that would enable her to require less assistance from others. Some of her grown kids would move into her place. They would help with some of the bills. She would get a part-time job. There were other elements of the plan as well.

She was very resistant to implementing these changes in her life. She struggled to see how they were helping rather than inconveniencing or even hurting her. Our meeting that evening was for me to gently remind her that the next check she would typically get would not be coming – as we had discussed for months. I spent considerable time rehearsing how I would deliver this message to her. It had to be done in a gentle, loving, and yet resolute way. It would have been so much easier for me to simply write her the check from donated funds. The church had the money. But, how long would this cycle go on? Every additional check would lead to another month this young woman would sit all day inside her home rather than seek to develop the willpower and work ethic that would lead to the satisfaction and accomplishment of supporting herself.

The meeting began and I softly delivered the news she had already heard from me before – there would be only one assistance check rather than two checks from the church this month. She began to sob. She was devastated. She reminded me I had access to funds that could help her. She was confused at what seemed like my lack of compassion. She sat slumped in the chair in front of me and felt tremendous pain from my decision.

After realizing my mind was made-up, she stood up and walked out of my office without shaking my hand or any pleasantries. I closed the door and cried. I knew what I had done was ultimately the best thing for this woman and her family, but I also knew it would be quite some time before she saw me as anything other than heartless. I was convinced my decision would positively impact the direction of this woman's life, but I knew it would take time – likely a long time – before she would see it that way.

The decision to lead others brings with it very difficult moments. In this opening chapter, I want to keep it real. Yes, leadership brings with it incredibly rewarding moments. We'll talk more about those in the pages ahead. But it also stretches and tests the leader in ways he or she has usually not experienced previously.

Leadership Means Making Decisions

Leaders make decisions. Those decisions are often unpopular. If everyone kept doing what they're doing right now, no one would ever deliver different results. Leaders facilitate movement. They help influence people to do things they're not currently doing so that the outcome will be different.

Leaders are not passive participants in an organization or on a team. I regularly sit through meetings and interact with a lot of managers who don't take a strong position on an issue being discussed. We pay leaders to make decisions. Groups don't make decisions. Leaders make decisions. The job of the group is to inform the leader so he or she makes the best decision possible.

Far too often, managers view their role as facilitating discussion or helping people do their jobs. That's part of it, but this view misses a critical element of leadership. When you decide to be a leader, you are choosing to put yourself into situations where you will need to make difficult decisions. It is your job to take a position – to choose a path or determine the course of action. Who you choose to surround yourself with will have a huge impact on the quality of your decisions. There is a balance that great leaders must strike between listening to the opinions of others and shutting off dialogue and confidently making a decision.

Some managers struggle to listen to others. They make decisions without listening to hardly anyone and not interpreting the decisions they make. Others listen to everyone for far too long and seemingly can't get up the nerve or confidence to make the decision.

Think of leadership in its most basic form. Every tribe or

group needs someone who is tasked with carrying the flag and leading the way. Groups of people rarely completely agree on anything, so someone must be chosen to decide the answers to important decisions. Because leadership involves choices, it brings louder criticism, second-guessing, doubts, and even discussions behind your back.

Deciding to lead immediately creates distance between you and the people you seek to lead. Leadership also enables growth, insights, and experiences that those unwilling to lead don't receive. Leadership allows you to see, hear, learn, and feel things you would never encounter if you didn't raise your hand and volunteer yourself as a leader.

Leadership refines individuals. It increases their capacity. It expands their influence and impact. It broadens their legacy. Being a leader is, honestly, awesome! There's nothing like making a significant impact on an organization's performance or another person's life.

If you answered Question #1 – *Do you want to be a leader?* – with a YES, then you're ready to head to chapter two now.

Sometimes the Timing Isn't Right

To those who answered Question #1 with a no, I appreciate your honesty. Perhaps you're overwhelmed with the demands of life right now, and taking on additional responsibility isn't something you can muster at this moment in your life. Don't beat yourself up over it. Your moment will come. And when it does, I hope you'll return to these pages and seize the opportunity to impact others in a broader way.

There is one last group I need to address before we move on to chapter two. Some of you want to lead but feel that someone else is holding you back. You want to contribute more to an organization, but when you've applied for a promotion to management, you were denied the opportunity or told to go gain more experience and wait your turn.

Listen to me closely. No one can stop you from deciding to lead! Yes, they can block you from the title or position you want in a company, but they cannot put you in a box. If they try, consider appropriate ways to contribute more broadly and significantly to the organization. If your well-intentioned and humble efforts are punished, then it may be time to consider another place to contribute in a more meaningful way.

Do not allow yourself to become resentful. Do not allow yourself to be stagnant. Bitterness and apathy don't look good on a leader. Use the opportunity to motivate yourself. Being denied an opportunity to contribute more significantly to an organization can be a gift. It can be the nudge that's needed to knock on another door and discover opportunities to have an impact you currently don't see or aren't considering.

**ACTION
ITEMS**

■ **Answer Question #1:** Do you want to be a leader? Obviously many of you are already managing other people but that doesn't make you a leader. Are you willing to truly lead them in the way described in this chapter?

■ Consider why you want to lead others in a more significant way. What's the payoff for you and them if you do? What would strengthening your leadership skills do for your career, personal life, and lifestyle?

■ If you are not yet in a management position at work or the organizatons you volunteer with start to strengthen your leadership muscles by volunteering for assignments, offering ideas and solutions, and connecting with as many people as possible. Learn as much as you can about the area you want to lead. Connect with as many people as possible so you have a broad group to call upon for ideas and feedback as you get opportunities to lead. You control whether people view you➤

as a leader. Start impacting their perception of you as a leader.

- Think about areas you are now demonstrating a "maintaining" mindset rather than a "leading" one. Where are you simply maintaining the status quo or managing processes or schedules but not truly leading others? Think about how you could show up differently to demonstrate true leadership.

"If your actions inspire others to dream more, learn more, do more and become more, you are a leader."

———

SIMON **SINEK**

Describe
the Destination

*b*efore I was a leadership coach and consultant, I spent nearly two decades in the media business. I led teams responsible for producing news, sports, and talk content. One of the assignments I was given was to turn around the performance of a group of radio stations our national broadcast company purchased in Phoenix, Arizona.

The premier station among the group was a news, sports, and talk station that at one point had dominated the airwaves of the Southwest United States. When we began our assignment, the station was a shell of its former self. It had been bought and sold multiple times, leaving the staff dizzy from all the changes. Competitors had taken advantage of the situation and launched a very public attack on the brand, leaving listeners believing they were losers if they tuned in.

Up until that point in my career, I had never led a turnaround project. I had only led teams achieving good results and helped take them to the next level. In this case, I was given a team that was producing dismal results. The ratings and revenue generated by this station were far below anything deemed acceptable by our company. It was my job to change this.

A few months after moving my family to Phoenix and beginning this new assignment, I realized I had inherited a royal mess. The turnaround was going to require a massive effort. It was going to take a few years, not a few months. The place needed to be completely rebuilt from the ground up. Part of the staff would have to be let go. An entirely new leadership team would need to be assembled, and much of the on-air talent and behind-the-scenes support staff would need to be replaced.

The magnitude of the project was daunting, and I wondered if I had what it took to accomplish the job. After considering if I could lead this project, I realized I knew what had to happen. I understood how the radio station needed to sound to generate high ratings – which would then create vastly improved revenues. I could hear in my head how this station should sound on the air.

I envisioned the type of leaders I needed to hire. I identified the types of on-air talent I had to recruit. I understood exactly what kind of changes were necessary. I had worked for radio stations with extraordinary ratings, so I knew what they sounded like. I knew what was required.

This brings me to the next question people must answer as they consider leading others.

 QUESTION #2
Can You See and Describe the Destination?

People use the term *leader* so loosely. They forget what the word really means. A leader isn't just telling people what to do for fun. A leader is leading a group somewhere – there must be a destination. One of my major observations in working with tens of thousands of leaders around the world is how few of them have actually pondered the future. Most of them have spent little to no time thinking about the destination they are supposedly trying to reach.

When I ask, "Can you see the future?" I am not trying to find out if you know this year's sales target. I am not asking if you know or have any ideas about the goals for this quarter or next. I'm getting at a much broader question.

Jeff Bezos says he asks the thousands of leaders in his company to not think in a three-year time frame, but rather a five-to-seven-year time frame. Why would he do that?

He is pushing the leaders he hires to visualize the future.

Do you know where you are taking this company, this division, this team? Can you see what success looks like in three years or seven years? When was the last time you sat down and spent some time pondering what that future looks like? When was the last time you started a meeting talking about the destination you can see in your mind?

Question #2 should actually be broken down into two questions. The first question is: "Can you see the future?" The second is: "Can you describe it to others in terms they understand and can rally around?"

While we're at it, let's add a third question to this theme: "Do you frequently, consistently, and intentionally describe the destination to others?"

Maintainers Versus Leaders

Think of the difference between a leader and a maintainer. A leader is leading people somewhere new. A maintainer is keeping people in the same place.

Often, when our firm gets on the phone or in the room with leaders we have not worked with before and we ask them where they want to take their company or team, they struggle to answer. They seem perplexed by the question. They ask for time to think about it before they have to respond. They are so focused on today and reacting to problems that they seem to have spent very little energy in long-term planning or thinking.

Mid-level managers or supervisors shouldn't excuse

themselves from this question. It does not just apply to senior executives. Yes, ideally the CEO and C-Suite should be communicating their vision of where their company is headed in the coming years, which then informs lower level leaders as they develop plans and visions with their teams to help accomplish that plan. However, the lack of a strong corporate strategy or roadmap does not give anyone else an out. Some of the most impressive leaders I have worked with have had responsibility for portions of a company. They've taken ownership of developing a vision of where they want to guide their team – and they describe it frequently. These are the leaders I most often see promoted. Their areas of stewardship are often the parts of the organization growing the fastest.

This vision of the future is best articulated by discussing what it means for the consumer, the patient, the member, the user, or the industry. It should be concise and take less than 30 seconds to articulate. A compelling vision of the future can be just a couple of sentences long. It generates passion and enthusiasm in those who hear it. It creates contagious energy. It makes people want to work harder and smarter. It makes them feel part of a movement, a cause, a larger purpose.

Most managers, or maintainers, are reactors. They spend their meetings talking about short-term problems without making any connection to how it will help facilitate movement toward the long-term destination. A leader doesn't view their job as simply putting together a schedule or putting out today's fires. They are more visionary than that. They view their role as helping point the organization in a certain direction and to motivate and inspire the team to overcome the obstacles blocking the path toward the destination.

For those of you who are reading this book not as a manager of a corporation or entrepreneur, but rather as the leader of people in a congregation or in a volunteer role, or as someone who is trying to make a difference in even one person's life, I hope you see the relevance of Question #2 to you. The most revered figures in any religious history understood this principle. They spent their time describing the future. They asked for obedience to certain moral or ethical codes or values, not for what it meant today or tomorrow, but because of how that behavior would impact the eternal soul of the believer.

The greatest leaders I've known have been able to describe what the future looks like and what it means to groups *and* to individuals. In one-on-one conversations, they have sought to expand people's vision. They have been very intentional in helping people think beyond the window of time they usually focus on. The narrower your vision, the bigger every problem appears. When we can broaden our view, huge issues turn into temporary detours or mistakes.

Great leaders help people expand their vision. They help individuals and organizations see their potential. They take advantage of every opportunity to help others consider what's possible. They inspire us. Exceptional leaders help make problems seem smaller and opportunities larger. They help individuals and teams see what they can become.

The Four Essentials

For those of you leading a team or organization, let's get more specific. When I ask, "Can you describe the future?" I'm really trying to learn if you have these four things in place:

1. **A purpose:** This is what you are trying to accomplish.

2. **A long-range target:** This is usually one key metric you are working toward achieving within 3-5 years.

3. **A set of cultural behaviors or values:** A set of 4-6 behaviors that describe the way we need people to think and act in order for us to achieve our long-range target.

4. **Annual key results:** This consists of 3-5 metrics that define success this year and feed up into the long-range target.

This may sound like a lot, but it's really quite simple. Here is an example to help you visualize what The Four Essentials look like in the real world.

I mentioned Jeff, who leads a food manufacturing company, in Chapter 1. His company is actually a joint venture between two larger companies, one based in the United States and the other in Mexico. They make things like frozen burritos, salsas, guacamole, and tortilla chips.

When Jeff took over the company, he realized it would be difficult to get the thousands of people who worked for his company to rally around making salsa or bean dip. This organization needed to exist for a bigger reason and success needed to be measured by something more than the number of bags of tortilla chips shipped. He and his team went to work on coming up with four things: a purpose, a list of cultural behaviors, a long-range target, and annual key results.

> PURPOSE:
>
> *To bring the spirit of Mexico*
> *into American homes*

This is the reason the company exists. Yes, they make burritos or salsa. But the *reason* they were making these products was to bring the spirit of Mexico into the homes of a nation whose population was becoming increasingly Latino and interested in Latino food and culture. You can't walk into one of this company's plants or offices without hearing someone mention this purpose. It's discussed in meetings. It's printed on agendas and PowerPoint slide decks. It's everywhere. Employees don't just see it and forget about it. This mission drives the organization. Everyone who works at the company feels responsible for achieving this purpose.

> LONG-RANGE TARGET:
>
> *$__ in Sales in 2025*

If you ask a factory worker, an employee in marketing, or

any manager what long-range target this company is working toward, they would all tell you $_ in sales in 2025. (They would actually tell you the real number. I'm not printing it here because, well, they wouldn't exactly want the whole world to know it.) Inside the company, you can't find anyone who hasn't heard the number. It's the first slide shown in any presentation at national sales meetings and leadership conferences. It's discussed in new employee orientation. People know this is the result their company plans to hit by 2025. Having that long-term awareness helps the leaders of the company quickly and simply describe the future. Every plant knows how they fit into the long-term higher revenue number.

As I write this book, I have been on the phone with the CEO of this company. We chat at least once a month to track progress on all four elements mentioned in this chapter. In the past two years, the company has increased sales by more than $100 million through organic growth.

A set of cultural behaviors or values

We need people to:

Deliver Excellence
- I am committed to excellence and do not accept mediocre performance

$\rightarrow$

Speak Right

- I say what needs to be said when it needs to be said

Solve It

- I proactively point out challenges and offer solutions

Fiesta Forever

- I promote a fun workplace where we accomplish our results

These statements are not worded exactly how this company wrote their cultural behaviors, but they are close enough to give you a sense of what made the list. The leadership team wrote these after considering how they needed the workforce to think and act in order to accelerate the achievement of the long-range target. Every company has a strategic plan. Few have a culture management plan. Companies like Amazon, Southwest Airlines, Apple, Chick-fil-A, Ritz Carlton, and Nordstrom are all very intentional in managing their culture in a way that creates a competitive advantage.

Many companies have values, but they are a list of words that someone wrote a long time ago and no one can recite from memory or even cares about. The word "values" has become so meaningless – or even negative – in most organizations that I generally don't like using it. Regardless of whether you call them values or cultural behaviors, the point is every team should have a list of how they need people to think and act in order for the company to fulfill its purpose and achieve its long-range target.

Jeff Bezos created this list in the early days of building Amazon. He calls them Leadership Principles. In Jeff's mind, every employee Amazon hires should be a "leader." Take a look at just a couple of the Leadership Principles Amazon uses to help employees understand how they need to think and act in order to meet Amazon's long-range target:

- **Customer Obsession**

  Leaders start with the customer and work backward. They work vigorously to earn and keep customer trust. Although leaders pay attention to competitors, they obsess over customers.

- **Bias for Action**

  Speed matters in business. Many decisions and actions are reversible and do not need extensive study. We value calculated risk-taking.

Those are just two of Amazon's Leadership Principles, or cultural behaviors. Think about how powerful it is to describe to employees how you want them to think and act. The principle, Bias for Action, is incredibly bold. It tells everyone throughout Amazon that speed is more important than extensive study. That isn't how every company wants their employees thinking, but it is how Bezos and his senior team want Amazonians thinking and acting.

A list of 4-6 critical behaviors defined by senior leaders of an organization, the owner of a small business, the manager of a team, or even a parent can be powerful. Our family actually has four cultural behaviors that we wrote during a long car ride. They describe how we need to think and act in order for our family of six to achieve the long-range target we have. (That's what happens when you have a dad who does this stuff for a living – the kids have to endure discussions about family cultural behaviors!)

ANNUAL KEY RESULT:

$___ million in sales, $___ in profit, and a ___% fill rate

Jeff's company has three Annual Key Results: a sales/revenue target, a profit number, and a factory fill rate goal. For your organization, the key results might include a safety metric, a customer satisfaction or NPS score, an employee engagement or retention number, or something totally different.

Every company has lots of metrics they're tracking, but for a group of people to function as a team, they must work toward shared results. Think of a football team tracking hundreds of statistics in a game. Each of those stats is important and needs to be measured and examined. But when the whistle is blown at the end of the game, the only statistic that really matters is the number of points on the scoreboard.

Many leaders complain about silos that exist in their organization, but the reality is most leaders have *created* those silos. They have done it by holding different departments accountable for different results, and by having no shared measures of success. In other words, the accounting department doesn't feel responsible for the revenue number. The marketing team doesn't measure its success by profit margin. The individuals in sales aren't consumed with overall personnel safety or employee retention numbers.

While each team and individual should have specific metrics they're watching very closely, they should also have accountability for the overall organization's Annual Key Results.

One of the biggest surprises I experienced when I shifted from leading my own team to consulting with leaders around the globe was how many organizations don't have clearly defined and understood Annual Key Results. The Key Results should be known by everyone in a company. Each employee should feel accountability to help achieve them. The Annual Key Results are described by leaders as a checkpoint on the way to the Long-Range Target. If a company only has Annual Key Results but misses defining and constantly describing the Long-Range Target, its leaders can't respond with a "yes" to Question #2: Can You See and Describe the Future?

Likewise, if a company only has a Long-Range Target but no Annual Key Results, then people don't know what the roadmap looks like. This makes it much more difficult to get a company or organization from where it is now to where it wants to be three to five years from now.

The way to make sure you're answering Question #2 with a *yes* is to define The Four Essentials – and make sure they are each reviewed continuously. Discuss these elements in meetings, on calls, in leadership conferences, during employee one-on-ones, in new team member orientation, in annual reviews or quarterly check-ins, etc. Having them defined takes a little time but is a critical step in effectively leading an organization to a destination it has not yet been. After defining them, it's critical that all four *permeate* an organization. When a leader gets tired of describing the future, it's likely his or her employees are finally hearing the message.

What I am describing here is not something I've made up. The list of companies that have found value in defining the future as I'm describing it here includes Amazon, Google, Spotify, Hormel, LinkedIn, Lockheed Martin, Disney, and Samsung. If I started citing research that shows how important defining these four essentials are, it would take up the rest of this book. I'll mention just one study. Deloitte – the management and leadership consulting firm – conducted a two-year study that showed NOTHING has more impact than "clearly defined goals that are written down and shared freely... goals create alignment, clarity, and job satisfaction."[1] (Doerr and Page, 2018)

Everyone Must Know the Destination

Great leaders understand that to take an organization where they want to go, they need as many employees as possible thinking about, understanding, and working toward that destination. It's not enough for the senior leaders or even mid-level managers to see the future. An effort needs to be made to get every employee aligned with where the organization is going. This only happens when leaders take the time to see and describe the future.

This principle applies just as much for nonprofits, religious organizations, and even families as it does for major corporations or small businesses. In our family, we've defined what our Long-Range Target as well as our Cultural Behaviors (Values).

As mentioned before, I have been a part of several leadership teams at the church I attend. I have noticed a major difference when those leadership teams have been intentional – constantly speaking to the purpose and short-term Key Results they're trying to deliver.

One of the great leaders in modern America understood the value of focusing people's attention on the future and describing for them what it looked like. When you read the words Rev. Dr. Martin Luther King Jr. chose to use in some of his most famous

---

[1] John Doerr and Larry Page, *Measure What Matters* (New York: Penguin Random House, 2018), 10.

and most mobilizing speeches, you realize how purposeful he was in helping others see the destination to which he was trying to lead them. He didn't just say someday everyone would be treated equally.

He described exactly what it would look like in powerful sensory language:

"I have a dream that one day on the red hills of Georgia, sons of former slaves and the sons of former slave owners will be able to sit down together at the table of brotherhood. I have a dream that one day down in Alabama…little black boys and black girls will be able to join hands with little white boys and white girls as sisters and brothers."[2]

On the day before he was fatally shot, he wanted to make it clear that he had seen the future:

"I've seen the Promised Land. I may not get there with you. But I want you to know tonight, that we, as a people, will get to the promised land. Mine eyes have seen the glory of the coming of the Lord!"[3]

Managers manage today. Leaders lead us toward tomorrow. Even as he was assaulted and watched his followers beaten as he battled a nation suspicious of his motives and unsure of what was to come, King was unrelenting in keeping his focus, not on

---

[2] King, Martin L., Jr. "I Have a Dream." Speech. Lincoln Memorial, Washington, D. C. 28 Aug. 1963.

[3] Ibid.

the struggles of his time but rather the promise of the future.

At Rice Stadium in Houston, Texas, President John F. Kennedy spoke to a huge crowd with the entire country as his true audience. He felt the need to describe the future:

> *The exploration of space will go ahead, whether we join in it or not, and it is one of the great adventures of all time, and no nation which expects to be the leader of other nations can expect to stay behind in the race for space.*
>
> *We choose to go to the moon.*
>
> *But if I were to say, my fellow citizens, that we shall send to the moon, 240,000 miles away from the control station in Houston, a giant rocket more than 300 feet tall, the length of this football field, made of new metal alloys, some of which have not yet been invented, capable of standing heat and stresses several times more than have ever been experienced, fitted together with a precision better than the finest watch, carrying all the equipment needed for propulsion, guidance, control, communications, food and survival, on an untried mission, to an unknown celestial body, and then return it safely to earth, re-entering the atmosphere at speeds of over 25,000 miles per hour, causing heat about half that of the temperature of the sun—almost as hot as it is here today— and do all this, and do it right, and do it first before this decade is out—then we must be bold.*
>
> *It will be done. And it will be done before the end of this decade.*[4]

President Kennedy could not only see the future, but he could also describe it. He understood the value of having an entire nation aware of that vision. In speech after speech, he took the time to describe the destination.

Ron Campbell was a star computer programmer in the 1970s who was heavily recruited by several early tech companies. Keep in mind, this was during the days when computers were huge machines, not yet devices owned by consumers. After being invited by Apple CEO Steve Jobs to lunch, Campbell asked him what his vision was of the personal computer. "For the next hour, [Jobs] talked about how personal computers were going to change the world. He painted a picture of how it would change everything about the way we worked, educated our children and entertained ourselves. You couldn't help but buy in," Campbell said.[5]

Leaders can see the future, describe it, and frequently speak about it.

---

[4] Kennedy's Address at Rice University on Space Exploration." *Archival Film.* 12 Sep. 1962. *NBC Learn.* Web. Accessed on March 4, 2019.

[5] https://www.forbes.com/sites/carminegallo/2011/01/18/steve-jobs-and-the-power-of-vision/#3d305fbb172b Accessed on February 28, 2019.

ACTION ITEMS

- **Answer Question #2:** Can you see and describe the destination?

- Utilize members of your organization to help you define The Four Essentials for your team. Involve your direct reports as well as a small group of people throughout your organization.

  - What is your team's purpose?

  - What is your long-range target?

  - What are your cultural behaviors or values?

  - What are your Annual Key Results?

- Roll out The Four Essentials to everyone in the organization. Do NOT do this in an email. The goal here is to get everyone aligned to them. Allow enough time in the meeting(s) where this will be rolled out for questions, comments, and observations from the group in the room.

→

- Consider where you can put
  elements of The Four Essentials
  so that people are bumping up
  against them and so they remain
  top of mind. Examples might
  be meeting agendas, signage,
  orientation, employee reviews,
  employee recognition, one-on-
  ones, etc.

- Practice regularly describing
  the destination – where the
  organization is headed and why it
  matters to the average employee
  and customer – to others in
  engaging and inspiring ways. You
  should be doing speaking about
  the destination constantly.

"Individuals don't win in business,
teams do."

———

SAM **WALTON**

Delegate & Motivate

*O*ne of the critical elements of the radio station turnaround project I talked about in the last chapter was assembling a leadership team that could help me pull off this difficult challenge. I spent considerable time and energy searching for the right leaders to join our team. We scoured the country and interviewed dozens of people. If we were actually going to pull off this difficult turnaround, we had to get the right people on the leadership team – from the very beginning.

One of the leaders we hired was one of the most committed people with whom I've ever worked. Let's call him Phil. Phil spent more time at work than anyone I have ever met. He usually arrived before 7 a.m., and it was not uncommon for him to head home after midnight. His dedication to the job was remarkable.

Phil could answer both of the first two questions of this book with a solid YES. He wanted to be a leader and had, in fact, *been* a leader at other organizations already in his life. Could Phil see the future? Absolutely. He shared my vision of where we needed to take this media property. I had absolutely no question that this individual could see the future clearly and describe it to others.

Phil helped our organization move forward. He accomplished so much. Yet, in one particular area, Phil struggled as a leader. It was such a critical area that it became clear Phil wasn't the leader who would be able to take us fully to where we needed to go. Several times I met with him and coached him on changes he needed to make in this one critical area, and he always responded that he would work on it. But he was never able to change in a meaningful way.

The challenge Phil had was delegating. He struggled tremendously in being able to train others how to do the things he needed them to do and in trusting them enough to give them space to fail or succeed – and then make necessary adjustments. That's why he worked such long hours. He was doing everyone's job. Phil was a man of tremendous character and dedication so he would not allow himself to go home until the job was done effectively. To Phil, that usually meant he needed to do it. There were very few things Phil didn't get involved in or touch directly. He considered it critical to be involved in everything to make sure things were done right.

As I watched Phil try to help our organization complete the turnaround we were hired to achieve, I noticed no significant upgrade in the level of talent he managed. The current staff continued to deal with the same challenges, and the new hires were about equal to who we already employed. Don't get me wrong. Phil had solid employees. These were very good people. But the talent pool we had in this area didn't show any signs of being significantly upgraded – which would end up being critical to our goal: producing better ratings and revenue.

The day Phil left, I was so bummed. He was well-liked; he was a workhorse. But he couldn't delegate. Phil would have answered the next crucial question with a "no" at that stage in his career.

QUESTION #3
Can You Delegate to & Develop Others?

This question exposes one of the most common shortcomings of leaders. Organizations usually promote exceptional individual contributors to management positions and then wonder why that person – who is such a hard worker and knows what needs to be done – is so ineffective in leading others. Often, it's because of Question #3. They have not learned how to delegate.

A critical shift must happen when a person goes from being

an individual contributor responsible for only what they do to being a manager accountable for the output of a team. When someone is promoted into management, they are no longer accountable for their personal output but rather for the output of their collective team. Many leaders struggle to make this transition.

To help understand why this change is so critical, think of a good employee as an engine. An engine propels an object like a car, plane, or boat forward. If it's a good engine, it can move that plane at a pretty high speed.

Most people think when they're promoted to a management position that only a few things have changed: their pay, where they sit, and how much they're responsible for. They fail to understand they need to make significant shifts in how they work. A new manager is no longer responsible for one engine, they are accountable for five or 10 or 20 engines. Again, their success is no longer measured by what THEY do, but rather by what their team does.

The amount of time you're spending working on something as a leader doesn't mean much. What truly matters is what your team is accomplishing. Phil was never able to fully grasp this concept while we worked together. His engine ran exceptionally well, but I knew he wouldn't be able to sustain his extremely intense schedule at work. The way to improve the performance of his team wasn't for him to stay longer hours and stress more. It was for him to learn how to delegate and increase the production of other engines in the organization that reported up to him.

Leaders who aren't great at delegating take too long to get organizations to the destination they visualize in Question #2. Sometimes leaders can see where they need to take a team, but they end up having to exit the organization early because their delegation skills are underdeveloped.

Delegation and Development in Practice

As we discussed in previous chapters, one of the organizations our firm works with is a 125-year-old food service company. You would recognize the brand name as it supplies numerous products to your local grocery store. A few years ago, they acquired a company that manufacturers Mexican food items including salsa and tortillas. The market for these types of foods is exploding in the United States, so the acquisition became a major growth arm for the parent company. When I first started observing and working with the leadership team of this Mexican food supplier, I noticed their CEO was a talented executive. He was truly impressive.

After I watched him lead several meetings with his core and expanded leadership teams, he asked me to give him some feedback and share my observations about things he could do more effectively. One of the things I had noticed was how strong his leadership skills were compared to those of his core executive team. They were all competent people. But this CEO was noticeably more effective in describing the future, reading a room, articulating areas of concern and actions that were needed, and listening and empowering others than those on his team.

I asked this CEO if he noticed any differences in his ability to do those things and the skills of his senior leadership team. He humbly acknowledged this was something that weighed on his mind. He felt frustrated. I told this CEO that for him to ever climb in the organization, he was going to have to elevate the skillset of these leaders. There could not be such a valley between his leadership approach and theirs.

He asked me, "How do I accomplish this?" I told him to pick one or two members of his team and get in the habit of frequently asking them the following question: "Why do you think I just did that?"

He could do this exercise with one of his senior executives after they watched him ask a particular question of a plant manager during a quarterly tour of the facility. After he got off the stage at a company leadership conference, he could pull aside one of his senior team members and ask them why they thought he showed a particular slide or focused on a specific idea during his presentation. He could call a member of his team after a Zoom meeting and discuss why he ran the meeting a certain way.

The point of asking his team these questions was to create an opportunity for this CEO to *explain why he does things the way he does them*. It's a knowledge transfer. I wanted him transferring some of what was in his head into the heads of a few other senior leaders. He needed to accelerate the rate of speed of his company by fine-tuning more engines – and not just rely on the production of his own. This is how you develop other leaders.

The Impact of Asking "Why Do You Think I Just Did That?"

This conversation took place in 2016. At the beginning of 2018, that CEO was promoted to a more senior position in the parent company. His VP of Sales – one of the members of his top team he had focused on developing – was given his former role. His promotion would never have happened if he had not delegated to and developed that member of his team. Other people in the corporation not only noticed the phenomenal results his company was producing, but they felt confident enough in the caliber of the members of his executive team to elevate one of them and not worry about an uncertain transition.

U.S. President Theodore Roosevelt said, "The best executive is the one who has sense enough to pick good men [and women obviously] to do what he wants done, and self-restraint to keep from meddling while they do it."

I was in Florida recently to meet with the leadership team of a well-known national restaurant chain. This chain is one of several household names that are owned by one of the largest restaurant companies in the world. As I walked through their global headquarters, I saw a sign that made me smile. The leaders of the parent company decided to put up on the walls – in large letters no one could miss – one of their expectations of leaders of this company. It said: "Leaders are also responsible for future leadership."

Some might read this message and think it means it is their job to recruit or hire future leaders. That's the easy part. The harder part is developing these individuals and delegating critical tasks to them.

Leadership author John Maxwell has said, "If you want to do a few small things right, do them yourself. If you want to do great things and make a big impact, learn to delegate."

What Delegation Really Means

When we talk about the importance of delegating to others, one question often comes up: delegate what? While delegating tasks is certainly part of what needs to happen here, I'm actually addressing something more critical. When I speak of delegation, I'm actually referring to two things:

- Recruiting others to take accountability to accomplish the results we spoke about in the last chapter.

- Delegating decision making to the lowest level possible.

Most employees measure their success by the amount of

activity they accomplish in a day or week. They view their job as a "to-do list" of tasks. If they get all of their tasks done, then they've done their job. The question becomes, "Who is gauging their success by whether or not the organization or team delivers the Key Results we spoke of in the last chapter?" In most companies, only the most senior leaders think about those Key Results on a daily basis.

In 1999, Silicon Valley investor John Doerr made a presentation to the leadership of Google. It was about something he had seen at Intel. The idea was a system called Objectives and Key Results, or OKRs. The idea is that the company has a few clear Objectives and Key Results that are meaningful and measurable. Then, every division and individual have their own set of OKRs that feed up into helping accomplish the company-wide set. The idea is that employees aren't paid to do activities. They are paid to help the company accomplish Objectives and deliver Key Results.

Too few leaders hold employees accountable for results. How do I know? Because of hundreds of conversations I've had with members of organizations in every kind of industry imaginable. The first time I speak with an executive I haven't worked with before, I ask her or him if I can interview a few members of their team. I always ask the same core set of questions during those interviews. One of the first questions is, "What are the Key Results or outcomes the organization is working to deliver this year?"

It seems like such a basic question, yet it is almost always answered with another question: "Russ, what do you mean?"

I typically explain it this way:

> *If I gathered about 15-20 members of the team in a conference room and asked them to help me generate a list of 3-4 bullet points on a whiteboard that represented the absolute most important results the organization must deliver this year, what are the 3-4 things the group would be aligned around telling me to write on the board?*

Most of the time, the response I get to that question is "I'd need to give that some thought," or, "That's a tough question to answer." This chapter's question, Question #3: *Can You Delegate to & Develop Others,* is broader than it appears. Delegating starts by understanding employees aren't paid to do tasks. They're paid to deliver results. Leaders who deliver sustained extraordinary results understand this and delegate achieving the results to everyone.

Once you've defined The Four Essentials discussed in Chapter 2, then it's time to start delegating or recruiting others to make them happen.

Awareness Versus Alignment

As you begin to broaden the discussion about results to all members of the organization, please understand the difference between making people aware of the Key Results and aligning people around them.

Most people in management positions are great at making people *aware* of things. Very few are skilled or experienced at getting teams *aligned* around things. Think for a moment about what a leader would do in a meeting in which they are seeking to build awareness around the organization's Key Results, versus what they would do in a meeting where the goal is building alignment around those KRs.

What would a leader do when the goal is awareness? Some of the responses to that question might be:

- Send out an email announcing the Key Results

- Call a meeting where they:

  * Announce the Key Results.

  * Show a PowerPoint deck that reveals the Key Results for this year versus what we delivered last year.

  * Hand out copies of the Key Results for people to put at their cubicles or on a badge buddy for their employee badge lanyard.

  * Ask if anyone has any questions about the Key Results.

Now, consider how that meeting would look if the goal was alignment around the Key Results. The leader would likely do some of the following:

- Everything listed above (except send an email!)

- Ask the team what questions they have around the Key Results. It sounds minor but there is a very big difference in a meeting when a leader quickly asks, "Do you have any questions?" versus one where the leader asks, "What questions do you have about these Key Results?" and then stands quietly looking at the team for 7-10 seconds of silence.

- Ask the team to consider how what they do impacts the Key Results and listen to a few responses.

- Seek pushback, critical questions, concerns, and general observations about the Key Results.

Those are two very different meetings. Great leaders intentionally create experiences that generate alignment around the Key Results as soon as they're defined. The failure to do so leaves most managers spending months trying to understand why people aren't aligned and then fixing the problem.

An organization that is aligned around The Four Essentials generates very different results than one that is simply aware of them. Leaders who deliver sustained extraordinary results view their job as building alignment rather than just awareness.

Spread Out Decision Making

One of the most common complaints I hear in organizations, as leaders seek to get alignment around the future destination, is the lack of authority employees feel to make decisions. The data shows millennials especially struggle in these kinds of teams. They want to work for organizations that feel flat. That means the average employee isn't too far removed from decision making. Old-school companies still feel like there's an ivory tower where the old white guys live in isolated luxury and occasionally send out pigeons carrying directives to all their minions.

A large global manufacturing organization I have consulted with for several years is battling this exact problem right now. In 2018, Amazon announced it was building two new corporate campuses. The world's largest online retailer has fully tapped out the engineer and developer talent pool in the Seattle area and is now moving to new locales to help it attract more talent.

The company we consult has locations in the markets Amazon has considered moving into, and is extremely concerned they are going to lose the battle to recruit talent because of how well Amazon has spread out its decision-making process. It's a very intentional part of their culture. One of Amazon's Leadership Principles (or cultural behaviors) is called "Bias for Action." The company defines it this way: "Speed matters in business. Many decisions and actions are reversible and do not need extensive study. We value calculated risk-taking."[6]

Amazon makes it very clear they want their employees to make decisions – and to not get stuck *analyzing* data but rather to have a bias for action. The manufacturing company I consult couldn't have a more opposite culture. Decisions take forever to be made. They have to be elevated up several levels because most people don't feel empowered to make any decisions. Employees feel like the organization is hierarchical, with a heavy top-down approach. This company is working hard to change its culture. It's proving to be difficult due to how many leaders struggle with what we're discussing in this chapter. Top-down decision making used to be how organizations functioned. The internet and the sharing economy changed all of that. The most talented parts of the workforce are not attracted to – and are increasingly leaving – companies where the leaders of teams don't spread out decision making.

If you're reading this and saying, "Are you expecting me to let *everyone* make all the decisions? That sounds like chaos and huge inefficiencies." I'm glad you spoke up. I'm not suggesting everyone makes any decision they want to make. I'm saying that great leaders delegate some decisions out to other people while reserving the most critical ones for themselves. Then, as decision-makers prepare to make a choice, they seek feedback and input from as broad a group as possible so that everyone feels like they're having some involvement in decisions. The opportunity to give input leads to ownership. When people don't feel like they've been given a chance to be heard in the decision-making process, they become disengaged.

This principle of delegation also applies in settings other

6 https://www.amazon.jobs/en/principles
Accessed on February 28, 2019.

than corporations. It's important to anyone leading a family, a community organization, or a congregation.

A few years ago, my wife was asked to serve as a member of a leadership team at the church we attend. Another woman was the one chosen as the head of the team, and she requested my wife be one of three other women who oversaw this particular part of the church organization. The leader was highly capable and dedicated. Her commitment was evident in the many hours of service she rendered and the deep level of love and concern she displayed for those she had stewardship over. My wife was anxious to help and make a difference. She would regularly attend leadership meetings where she volunteered her time and energy, yet she consistently came home with no assignments or tasks to complete. She felt under-utilized.

It didn't appear the leader of the team had concerns about the capability of her team members to complete tasks. So, why did she so often assign all the tasks to herself? I realized she likely felt guilty delegating to others. Her motives were pure – she didn't want to take up their time. But that's too bad because the reality was that this team could have gotten even more done if its leader had approached things differently. She could have helped prepare any of those other women, including my wife, for future leadership roles had she viewed part of her job as developing other leaders.

The job of a leader is to not only help the organization achieve the results it needs to deliver now, but to accelerate movement toward future results. That cannot be done effectively without leaders who develop and delegate. Great leaders must not only answer Questions #1 & #2 with a YES. They must be able to answer Question #3 with a YES, too.

More Tips for Developing Others

- Delegate running a meeting to other people. Just because you're the senior leader in the room doesn't mean you should run every meeting.

- Encourage high potentials or future leaders to frequently speak up in meetings when questions are asked by the team. It shouldn't just be you – the senior leader – answering questions or reinforcing what your team needs people to do.

- Be liberal in publicly recognizing good decisions. Great leaders take credit for as few ideas and decisions as possible. They build trust in key members of their team so they can elevate them later and people will understand why.

- Give private and frequent constructive feedback to high potentials and future leaders. Help them see what they can do even better. Coaches constantly look for ways they can help good players become great players. Invest time to look for and communicate ways others can be even better. and ask them for constructive feedback for yourself as well!

- Praise members of your team to your boss, or bosses. People who develop a reputation for being skilled at developing others are frequently promoted faster. Make it clear to your boss how you're developing high potential members of your team. Their development makes you look stronger.

ACTION ITEMS

- **Answer Question #3:** Can you delegate to & develop others?

- Ask the people you are leading, "Why do you think I just did that?" Make a habit of sharing why you do what you do and how you think about problems and solutions.

- Delegate tasks regularly. Have others run some of your meetings. Assign some decisions to others. Delegate the project lead role to someone else. Invite someone down the org chart to attend your next offsite or leadership meeting. Go to lunch with a small group of individual contributors and ask them a ton of questions.

- Let people fail and fix their mistakes on their own. It's the only way they'll grow and become better leaders.

- Start to view your role as building other leaders. Investing time in creating more leaders pays off as it accelerates progress towards the results you want to achieve personally and the team needs to deliver collectively.

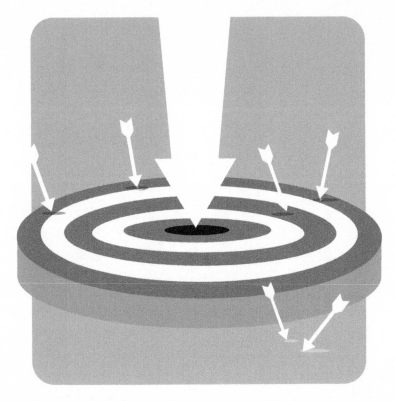

"Adhere to your purpose and you will soon feel as well as you ever did. On the contrary, if you falter, and give up, you will lose the power of keeping any resolution and will regret it all your life."

ABRAHAM **LINCOLN**

04

Determine to
Stand Alone

*a*s our team got deeply involved in leading the turnaround of the radio stations our national media company purchased in Phoenix, I faced a difficult situation. After I got our leadership team largely in place, we began replacing on-air personalities. Some of the most critical decisions we had to make were who we would put on the air in critical talk show host positions. I spent hours and hours listening to talk shows in other cities across the United States. I worked with consultants and headhunters to find just the right personalities that I felt would generate huge ratings among the demographics we were targeting.

One of my first hires was a talk show host from Dallas, Texas. He worked at a second-tier radio station in this larger media market but had the political views, energy level, experience, and on-air presence our station needed. He would absolutely put us back on the map. So, I flew him and his wife out to Phoenix, put them up in one of Arizona's swankiest resorts, and took them to an Arizona Diamondbacks game. I thought I wanted to hire him before I met him in person, and his visit to Phoenix convinced me I was right.

He eventually agreed to join our team, and after several months, debuted on our station. Immediately, he began generating noise in the market. He got noticed and ratings began to soar.

Then, something awful happened. He was hit by another car while driving home one night and suffered a brain injury. I will never forget how I felt when I visited with him and discovered he could no longer host a live, three-hour daily talk show. My plan to turn around this station had been dealt a huge blow. Not only that, but this man who had become a friend was now suffering through the darkest moments of his life.

As I was dealing with this huge personal and professional trial, one of the senior executives of our company made his quarterly visit to our market. He was a well-connected, successful, and very intense man. He was one of those executives who intentionally utilized intimidation as a leadership tactic. Don't get me wrong, I respected him, and he was an exceptional leader who had an indisputable record of delivering results. But he was also someone who made sure you knew who was in charge.

After a group dinner one night, this executive vice president of our company asked me if I could give him a ride back to his hotel. He was staying at the eclectic Valley Ho Hotel in Old Town Scottsdale. As we approached the hotel, he asked me to pull over on a side street. I shifted my SUV into park. He then turned to me from the passenger seat and said something to the effect of, "Russ, I hope the plan YOU have chosen to turn around these radio stations works. I like YOU and I really hope this plan of YOURS is the right one. As you know, YOU don't have all the time in the world, so at some point soon it will need to be obvious that YOU have succeeded in choosing the right course for us."

It was obvious he had intentionally chosen not to use any words like "us," "we," "team," or anything remotely plural in this conversation. He was making it clear this was totally about me and MY plan. It wasn't hard to read between the lines and understand his intent in this conversation. He had some doubts about the plan WE were executing, and he wanted me to know that I – and I alone – owned it.

As soon as he made those comments, he told me to go ahead and drop him off at his hotel. My drive home that night was about 20 miles, which took about 30 minutes. But it felt like forever.

The entire drive home, I sweated. I couldn't stop thinking of what the EVP had said. Here I was in the midst of dealing with an entirely unforeseen challenge – a challenge that would certainly delay the turnaround – and instead of consoling me, this executive wanted to make sure I knew my job was riding on whether my plan worked or not.

This story leads me to the next question regarding what it takes to be a great leader:

 QUESTION #4
Are You Willing to Stand Alone?

There are a few reasons we elevate the status of leaders in organizations and in our society. Leaders generally make more money and enjoy additional benefits or perks than everyone else in an organization or on a team. One of the reasons for this is they take on additional responsibility for the success or failure of an organization. They live or die, so to speak, by their decisions.

I love the saying that some credit to a senator in the Roman Empire from around 87 AD. JFK also liked to use it: "Victory has 100 fathers. Defeat is an orphan."

I've heard the maxim modified a bit as "Success has a thousand fathers. Failure is an orphan." The wording doesn't really matter – both versions are completely accurate. When success or victory occurs, everyone wants to claim they were a part of making it happen. Conversely, when failure or defeat happens, everyone runs for the exits and points fingers of blame.

Every leader will experience failures. They'll make the wrong decisions. Their plans will sometimes not work. In those moments, the leader, alone, will bear the brunt of it. It's part of the reason why the average lifespan of a CEO at an organization is around three years. A head coach in the NFL averages four seasons with a team. From 2013-2016, 19 NFL teams changed head coaches. Were all those coaches miserable leaders? No. But when the team didn't perform the way the owners and fans wanted, someone had to answer for the failure.

President Barack Obama was once asked about the nature of his job as President of the United States. He said, "I used to describe the nature of the presidency as having to make decisions about issues that nobody else could solve or are basically insolvable or at least not perfectly solvable," he said. "By definition, if a problem had an obvious solution to it, somebody else would have solved it before it got to me."

Isn't that true of any leader in any organization? The job of a leader is to make decisions. The decisions that come to you are the decisions that could not easily be made lower on the org chart. The more senior a leader, the more impact those decisions tend to have. Whenever someone makes a decision, they instantly alienate themselves. Decisions require a choice between multiple options, and almost always there are differing opinions in organizations about which option is best. No matter the choice the leader makes, someone is going to think it's the wrong one.

Why is leadership lonely? Because people will disagree with what you say and do sometimes. Those who vocally criticize some of your decisions will occasionally be people you counted as loyal supporters or friends. In moments when your decisions end up leading to undesired outcomes or create controversy, you will find the crowd of supporters around you has vanished and you are left standing alone. At that moment, you will experience the refining fire of leadership. Some react with bitterness or retreat.

Great leaders are not surprised by criticism, doubting, second-guessing, or even abandonment. They stand strong when their team experiences temporary setbacks.

Jeff Bezos said, "If you can't tolerate critics, don't do anything new or interesting."

Bezos didn't say you have to like critics. He said we need to tolerate them. I'm amazed at how many "leaders" are uncomfortable with people disagreeing with, or challenging, their decisions.

Are You Confident? Have You Taken a Clear Position?

You can't be a great leader without being willing to stand alone. In the example I've been using throughout this book, I had to make a decision when I drove away from dropping off that senior vice president at his hotel. I had to decide if I was confident in my plan. I had to decide if I was willing to stand up and say it was the right game plan – and be willing to accept the blame and consequences that would occur if it did not work.

In my career leading media properties, I often paid for research to be done on our on-air personalities. We would pay a company to call hundreds of radio listeners and ask them questions about our talk show hosts. If the talk show host didn't generate a decent amount of what we called "unfavorable" reviews, then I knew the host wasn't going to be successful. You wanted the "favorable" reviews to outnumber the "unfavorable," but if we didn't have about 15-25% of radio listeners who didn't like our talk show hosts, we knew they weren't generating enough of a reaction to drive high ratings.

I laugh when people get upset at the strong conservative political opinions personalities on Fox News Channel have or the liberal rantings of hosts on MSNBC and CNN. Those strong positions that make some people mad are put on the air by design. The hosts will quickly lose their jobs if they don't generate enough "unfavorable" reviews. Why? Because research shows that when someone takes a position, it causes a reaction in the audience. When a radio or television personality says "Donald Trump is a terrible president," that strong statement forces you to make a decision: do you agree or disagree? When you have to take a position as a listener or viewer, you are much more engaged in the program. Your emotions have been triggered. You're mad that personality said such a thing about Mr. Trump, or you're thrilled that someone else – besides just you – thinks he's bad for the country.

When someone takes a position, it becomes a line in the sand. People must decide whether they agree or disagree with it. Leaders are paid to take positions.

Sure, leaders should do their best to help get people aligned to why they made the decision they did. Great leaders seek to involve as many people as possible in the discussions that precede the decision. But regardless of all of that, a leader should still anticipate that some portion of their employees, their shareholders, their vendors, and ultimately, their customers will disagree with the decision. Great leaders must, in the words of Bezos, tolerate this. They should expect it.

Cycles of Success and Failure – and Loneliness

No leader will consistently be celebrated or even appreciated. Every leader at every level goes through cycles of success and failure. The successes feel good and yet are so often short-lived. The failures hurt. Before anyone Decides to Lead, they need to have clarity around the reality that the decision to be a leader will bring with it lonely days. Failure is hard for anyone, but the difficulty and the pain are magnified 10X for leaders. They stand on stages with bright spotlights on them. When they say something foolish or make an unwise decision, they do it in full sight of everyone.

The more successful the leader, the more intense the pain of each failure. Great leaders understand this risk. They are aware there will be days, months, and even years when they will have to push through criticism and loneliness. Several years ago, the man who was the leader of The Church of Jesus Christ of Latter-day Saints stood before a crowd of more than 16,000 students at Brigham Young University in Provo, Utah and decided to throw out his scripted speech. Instead, he delivered a remarkable discourse he later titled "The Loneliness of Leadership."

In that speech, Gordon B. Hinckley said, "The price of leadership is loneliness." He quoted William Shakespeare when he wrote, "Uneasy lies the head that wears a crown." (*King Henry IV, Part II,* Act 3, Scene 1, Line 31).

Forgive me for being so dark in this part of the book. After reading this chapter, some of you may think, "Who would ever want to put up with any of that?" It is not my intent to scare anyone out of pursuing being a leader in any aspect of their life. But as I consider the choices a person must make when Deciding to Lead, this book would not have been complete without covering this topic. As I have repeatedly stated, leadership brings with it incredibly rewarding experiences. It increases a person's capacity. It unlocks learning and joys of life that are not possible without being a leader. However, I want to be clear: along with the incredible highs of being a leader come tremendous lows.

Beware the Weathervane

Occasionally, managers try to escape the loneliness of

leadership by becoming a weathervane or windsock. Think of the old-fashioned weathervanes that used to be placed on top of barns and buildings. They pointed the direction the wind was blowing, just like the bright orange windsock you see next to a helipad where helicopters land at hospitals or airports.

Managers who choose to be a weathervane are those who decide that whatever direction the wind is blowing in their organization is the direction they are going to point. You've seen this happen. This is the manager who sits in meetings and quickly abandons supporting a proposal or idea if they sense it isn't popular. They rarely fight for anything. They tell you they want to promote you, but then pretend they never had this conversation when their boss shows some resistance to elevating your status in the company.

I once worked for a leader who could never say no. Everyone on the team thought they were just a few weeks away from a promotion. Everyone thought the boss agreed with them. Everyone thought the idea they brought up was about to be implemented. After a while, we all realized none of it was going to happen. We weren't going to be promoted. Our ideas weren't going to be implemented. And, he actually *didn't* think everything we said was correct. The amount of disengagement on that team was huge because, after a while, everyone knew that leader couldn't be trusted. What he said carried little weight. You knew he was simply giving you lip service. Our respect for him went down because he couldn't say no or challenge anything that was brought to him.

Members of an organization I'm working with currently frequently tell each other, "Whoever gets to [CEO's name] last is the one who will get their way." What they mean is the leader of their company is easily persuaded to change course or change his mind, depending on who is in the room with him at the time. He seemingly agrees with everyone in an effort to not cause problems or hurt feelings. His indecisiveness or lack of clear direction is causing that organization huge amounts of lost revenue and earnings due to the inefficiencies of his leadership style.

I have wondered why seasoned professionals – experienced leaders who should know better – sometimes lack clear direction and turn with the wind. Perhaps some of them were bolder earlier in their careers and experienced some of the loneliness of leadership we've discussed in this chapter. Maybe they have since decided they never want to experience it again. So, they rarely stick out their necks. They don't want to try anything bold. They figure out which direction the wind is blowing and point that way. Unfortunately, this is costing them and their organizations. These managers cannot answer Question #4 with a YES.

Standing Alone Shouldn't Last Long

As I write this chapter, I am concerned some people may interpret it incorrectly. To illustrate my concern, let me share a story from a Fortune 50 company we work with that does more than $50 billion in annual revenue. They employ tens of thousands of people around the globe.

We have worked with this company for several years and know it well. During one of our discussions with their senior executives, they voiced frustration with some tension that existed between two teams inside one of their divisions. One team was responsible for sales. The other was responsible for managing the projects the sales team sold. Frankly, the two teams didn't have a lot of nice things to say about each other. I discovered this during a series of more than a dozen interviews with the leadership teams of both departments.

Within a few minutes of beginning a call with the head of the project management team, he began telling me a long story. It involved a deal the sales team had done many years ago that turned out to be a disaster for the company, costing it more than $100 million in write-offs. Clearly, the sales team had made a huge mistake. As I sat on the phone in my home office listening to this lengthy story, I wondered why this leader had chosen to tell me about something that had happened so long ago.

It became clear he did not trust the sales team. That experience several years earlier was so bad he couldn't get over it. The reality was most of the current sales leadership team wasn't around when that terrible deal was done. Yet, this head of the project management team couldn't let go of it. He was bitter. He didn't trust the sales department. He intentionally created obstacles for them. He knew he wasn't liked by them or their leaders and he wore the dislike as a badge of honor. He, and he alone, was going to protect this global company from the sales team.

We went onsite and facilitated a meeting between the leaders of the sales team and the project management team. This leader I'm speaking of acted like a bully during the entire meeting. He created negative experiences for everyone. On purpose. Our desire was to help move the culture forward, and yet this leader was single-handedly holding it back. How do I know it was just him causing the problems? Well, because of what happened about six months later.

I was at a meeting in another part of this organization one day when someone from HR came up to me and said, "Russ, did you hear what happened when [that leader] retired a few months ago?" I responded that I wasn't up to date on the latest developments. She explained that the problem between the two teams was pretty much gone. She went on to share how well they were working together and how much the culture had improved – all because one individual was no longer around.

In a chapter where I talk about how leaders have to be willing to stand alone, it's important to be clear on how that loneliness should be temporary. That leader prided himself on standing alone – on being the only one willing to make sure the sales team was kept in check. Unfortunately, he had become the problem.

Sometimes we as leaders make decisions that are wrong. Sometimes we fail to see things because they pop up in our blind spots. Sometimes we hold onto beliefs far longer than we need to and they're actually weakening our ability to lead a team or organization.

If you find yourself consistently the only one in the room who holds a certain view, one of two things are true. Either you're wrong or you're in the wrong organization. Great leaders need to be confident and firm on the destination to which they're leading their teams, and they need to be willing to stand their ground when others question or doubt their decisions. But they also need to be humble enough to admit when they're wrong or when an organization doesn't want to continue to move in the direction they are pointing.

At those moments, a great leader will seek to understand why others feel differently than she does, reassess the facts on the ground, and then determine if they can get aligned with the direction their boss, the customer, the shareholders, or the team wants to go in. If they can't, then it's time to step aside and allow someone else to hold the flag and lead the team in the desired direction.

Great leaders need to be willing to stand alone sometimes, but if they consistently find themselves the only one charging up a certain hill, it's probably time to acknowledge reality.

I felt strongly about putting Question #4: *Are you willing to stand alone?* in this book because I want every leader to realize they aren't the only one to experience moments of testing and refinement. Anyone who has ever stood up, raised their hand, and volunteered to lead others goes through these periods from time to time. The greatest leaders who we collectively honor often earn their place in history due in part to their resolve in moments of testing and challenge. On the small stage I have played on in my life, these moments have been incredibly challenging. I wish I had been more prepared for them. I have not handled them perfectly. I want all of you to perform better than I have when you find yourself facing these moments.

Hopefully, you are seeing the picture of leadership I'm painting in this book. Great leaders stand for something. They can see the future and describe it. They are willing to develop and delegate to others in pursuing that future destination. And they are willing to stand alone in moments when a tough decision is required, and on occasions when it turns out some of their toughest decisions were wrong.

I'm so grateful I hired the talk show host I mentioned at the beginning of this chapter. Even though he was on that radio station far less time than I had hoped due to his brain injury, he changed the trajectory of that station. I'll share more about how that story ended in the pages ahead, but allow me to give you a quick update about the host.

He now lives on the Carolina coast with his wife and continues to battle the effects of a traumatic brain injury. Though he was never able to return to the airwaves, he is alive, active, and happy. Hiring him was a great decision that helped our station get its footing and begin to generate momentum. He was a critical part of our rebuilding mission. But the decision to hire him also brought unforeseen lonely moments for me – and profoundly altered his life and the lives of his family. I'll forever be grateful for his willingness to take a chance to help me, and my team, rebuild that Phoenix radio station. He injected so much confidence into our organization at a critical moment and helped us achieve something remarkable.

ACTION ITEMS

- Consider your authentic response to **Question #4: Are you willing to stand alone?**

- Get the perspective of others on your ability to make decisions and stick to them. Have you set a clear course? Are you willing to make the important and necessary decisions, or do you leave things ambiguous?

- Think of a decision you've made in the past that left you standing alone. What was the price you paid for making that decision – personal or professional? What did you, your team, a customer, or someone else gain from your willingness to stand up for that decision?

- Examine whether you've acted like a weathervane in the last 2-3 months. Were there any instances where you failed to defend an important decision or left your team feeling abandoned? What was the cost you – or others – paid?

"Servant leadership is all about making the goals clear and then rolling your sleeves up and doing whatever it takes to help people win. In that situation, they don't work for you; you work for them."

———

KEN **BLANCHARD**

The Bonus
Questions

*W*ait, there's more? Yes! I have more questions I want to ask you.

I believe the path to being a great leader begins with the four simple yet powerful questions we've discussed in this book. Answering these four questions with a *YES* will help you and your team get on the path to achieve extraordinary results. How do I know this? Because I have seen it play out over and over again in industry after industry.

I have purposefully left each chapter of this book relatively lean. I find I am more willing to read, consider, and implement ideas from a book if it doesn't take me too much time to read or keep repeating the same ideas over and over again. One of the reasons I didn't go with a mainstream publisher for this book is because friends of mine have been told by their publishers to write filler material just to meet the publisher's word count quota so a book "seems" more substantive. Do you know how much time I have wasted trying to dig and find value in a book after the first few chapters? You do because it's happened to you. That's insane.

I purposefully kept the chapters about half the size of those found in "normal" business books. The power of a good book is not in the words on the page but the pondering it generates within you – and ultimately, the actions this pondering inspires. This notion has driven me as I have written this book. Forgive my rant but I try to be transparent and real.

I hesitate to include an additional chapter that adds anything beyond the four questions, as I do not want to diminish the importance of those critical concepts. I hope you will spend time making sure you can answer the four questions with a YES, and that you will ask members of your team, your peers, and your family and friends for their perspective on those questions relative to you.

Some of the questions will generate a firmer YES than others. I'd encourage you to focus on the areas in which you might be deficient and spend time doing the things necessary to help you answer with a more resounding YES.

Being a great leader obviously doesn't end with your ability to say YES to just four questions – it's simply where great leadership *begins.* There are many more questions that define how skilled someone becomes at leading teams.

This chapter features four additional queries that originally hit the cutting room floor. However, that doesn't mean they aren't important. In fact, some of you might think one of these questions is *more* critical than some of the previous four. Every situation is different. Some of you lead nonprofits, volunteer organizations, or religious congregations, and in your area of influence, one of the extra questions posed in this chapter may be absolutely crucial.

Each of these questions deserves much more consideration than we have space or time for in this book. I present them here simply as additional food for thought for individuals who want to become great leaders. Unlike the main four questions, these are presented in no particular order.

QUESTION #5
Are You Willing to be a Servant Leader?

Every job has aspects that aren't very enjoyable. If you were to ask me what parts of my job consulting leaders of organizations I dislike the most, it would be dealing with arrogance. I'm not talking about confidence here. Confidence is absolutely critical to leadership. Leaders without confidence cannot be transformative. They are maintainers whose hesitant style leads to inefficiencies as people wait too long for decisions.

But great leaders balance confidence with humility and vulnerability. In fact, great leaders *intentionally create experiences* to demonstrate their humility and vulnerability. I was impressed to learn servant leadership is required of senior executives in the popular and successful Chick-fil-A restaurant company. In her book about her time as the head of HR at the chicken chain, Dee Ann Turner shares what her fellow members of the senior leadership team did to make sure they were demonstrating servant leadership in interactions with employees:

"Leadership is a tremendous responsibility to not only lead but also to serve those we lead," Turner writes. "In my organization, it is embedded into our culture that leaders are the first to arrive and the last to leave. Leaders ensure that everyone is served before serving themselves."[7]

I desperately wish I ran into more executives who are trying to be servant leaders. I see it more often in mid-level managers, but even there it isn't the norm. It takes boldness and confidence for someone to be promoted within an organization to a senior level. It can be hard for someone who must maintain a confident persona to balance that with actions of humility and serving others.

---

[7] http://purplegoldfish.com/gotta-serve-somebody/ Accessed July 6, 2018.

I could write so much more about this topic and may even do an entire book on it in the future. In the companies or divisions of a company where I have seen servant leadership, there is a remarkably strong culture. Employees of servant leaders rarely just clock in and clock out. They tend to be more devoted and committed to an organization. People work hard for money, yet they work harder for a good boss – especially one they believe doesn't place himself or herself above others.

QUESTION #6
Are You Allergic to the Status Quo?

I debated including this question because it might seem so similar to Question #2: *Can You See and Describe the Destination?* But it is absolutely a different question. I have worked with organizations where the executives can see and describe the place they want to take everyone, but they lack urgency in getting there.

If you were to ask me about the biggest surprises I experienced during years of walking into dozens of companies and working with thousands of leaders around the world, this question would get at the heart of one of them. I have been shocked to discover how many managers and executives lack the urgency to achieve better results. Don't get me wrong here. I'm not saying they don't *want* better results. I'm saying they don't act like they are allergic to the status quo. They don't have a fire in the belly. They aren't overflowing with passion about where they want to take their team.

It's amazing how many managers are really just maintainers. I wonder how many of them realize that with just a few of the tweaks discussed in this book – if they could really even answer two or three of these questions with a YES – they could change everything. Doing so would lead to more opportunity for them in their existing company, or somewhere else.

One of the coolest parts of my job is seeing teams accomplish things they didn't think were possible. I get to see organizations blow past their old performance levels and achieve remarkable things. In every instance in which this occurs, Question #6 could be answered with a loud YES in those organizations. The leaders view themselves as coaches walking into a locker room helping a team realize they can actually win the game – they can be the champs. There is no confusion amongst their team about how the leader feels about slow growth. It just wouldn't be acceptable.

One of the CEOs I've worked with for the last few years, and come to deeply respect, once said to me, "There is no question that whatever three things we put into our annual Key Results, we will achieve." I couldn't believe his confidence. No player ever bats 1000. Everyone gets strikes at the plate or loses some games. But in three years of watching him closely, the truth is his organization of 4,000 people has never missed one of their annual Key Results. The reason for this is simple: in his organization, there is a complete determination that employees must find a way to make it happen.

If you are satisfied with slow growth, or okay with your team inching along and getting somewhat close to your revenue, safety, retention, engagement, or customer service numbers, then you likely aren't viewed by others as a great leader.

QUESTION #7
Are You Willing to Change?

If you are to become a great leader, a year from now you will be different than you are right now. Five years from now, you'll lead very differently from how you do at this moment. Great leaders are curious. They realize they don't have all the answers. Being a great leader does not mean you have to be the smartest person in the room.

I remember how timid my wife felt and acted when she was promoted to be an Area Sales Manager for the retail company she worked for right out of college. We were young and had little life experience. The company my wife worked for saw leadership potential in her and wanted her to lead a team consisting of individuals who were almost all older than she was at the time. I'm sure some of you younger readers of this book can relate to this experience. She looked around her team and was intimidated by the experience, maturity, and age of her employees. Over time, she gained confidence as she realized how much they respected her – and loved working for her.

Great leaders realize they don't have to be the smartest, most capable, or most experienced person on the team. Sometimes

I've seen managers purposefully not hire someone because they feel threatened by an applicant's experience, even when that person seems to have adequate humility. I've worked alongside people at church who are clearly intimidated by the mere presence of members of the congregation who have more leadership experience than they have.

Great leaders present themselves as the decision-maker, the tour guide. They see themselves as the one whose current assignment is to point a group or team where it needs to go. They know it is their job to help the group or team overcome the obstacles that lie ahead on the path.

When leaders view themselves this way, they realize it is okay to acknowledge they are imperfect and are learning and improving on the job. They understand that to get other people to change and improve the way they are doing things, they, as the leader of the team, must set the tone of personal and professional improvement.

I've been consulting one of the largest health insurance companies in the United States for several years. When they first called and hired us to work with them, they asked us to meet with a team of ten executives in a high-rise in downtown Philadelphia one evening. Our meeting started after the sun had already gone down.

To say this group of executives was frustrated with one another would be a huge understatement. The air was filled with tension as we were led into the room where we would be meeting. We had been called in because the future of the company was jeopardized by the discontent between these executives and the teams they led. An organization that employed tens of thousands of people, and provided health insurance for millions of Americans, was suffering through a very rough spell because some of these ten executives didn't respect one another.

We asked the three most senior leaders in the room to begin the meeting by making some brief opening comments. The first two executives got up and spoke about how they hoped this meeting would help solve some of the challenges their teams were having working together.

Then, the head of sales stood up and walked to the front of the small room. He faced the semi-circle of chairs where the rest of the executives sat. The words he spewed cannot be published in a family-friendly book.

He spoke about how he resented having to fly in to attend this meeting. With expletive-packed sentences, he spoke of how the problems the company was facing were the fault of the others in the room but not him or any of his team. The longer he spoke, the worse it got.

I sat in the back of the room struggling to hide my shock at his behavior. I will never forget the moment. After the sales executive finished blaming everyone and taking no accountability for any part of the company's challenges, he returned to his seat and our team stood up. I'm not going to lie – we had some serious concern over how the next few minutes were going to go. We couldn't allow the comments that had just been made to stand. And yet we had absolutely no relationship with these executives. This was our first time meeting them. We were there at the direction of their boss – who had opted not to attend.

Over the course of the next hour, we started talking about culture. We shared some of our experiences and worked hard to build credibility and trust with each person present in a manner appropriate for the moment. We respectfully pushed and challenged the group. We spent a day and a half with that team locked away in a room high above downtown Philadelphia. At the end of the second day, the head of sales stood up and made some closing comments to the group. He is a private man who tends to speak only when asked or when he feels he can no longer maintain his silence.

As he stood, I held my breath. This time, there were no four-letter words. He spoke softly. He talked about how much value he had found in the time this small group had spent together over the previous day and a half. He talked about how he had discovered he was part of the problem and that he was going to work hard to change and help his team change some of the experiences they were creating for the other departments represented in the room.

It's been several years since that meeting. The words from that sales executive were not hollow. As I reflect on our experiences of working with this company, I am frankly amazed at how much this leader has adjusted how he leads. He has since been promoted and now oversees a huge portion of that growing public company. His willingness to change literally impacted tens of thousands of people down the org chart as well as the level of service millions of Americans are receiving from their health insurance company. I have a huge amount of respect for this leader. He's far from perfect, like every leader, but he's a much stronger leader than he was a few years ago.

I have been surprised at how few leaders I have worked with over the last several years are actively working on adjusting how they lead to meet the changing workforce, market conditions, and customer demands. Sure, most leaders *say* they want to improve. And yet, when I ask leaders what specific adjustments or changes they've made in the last month based on constructive feedback they've received, I usually get blank stares and long pauses.

Leaders must seek regular and specific feedback from their teams, and then communicate on a regular basis the changes they're making based on that feedback. When a leader stands in front of her team and humbly acknowledges the things she is learning, the ways she is seeking to be a better leader, and the changes she is making in policies, procedures, and systems based on feedback she's received, it dramatically impacts the culture of a team. It leads to an environment where a desire to improve is part of the culture from top to bottom.

QUESTION #8
Are You Able to Shut Off the Noise?

I was describing to my kids recently what it was like to be a teenager when cell phones, texting, Netflix, YouTube, apps, Google Maps, email, and Amazon didn't exist. They looked at me with an expression that said, "Dad, how did you and Mom even survive during those dark days of history?" The more I talked, the more I realized just how much life truly has changed in just a couple of decades.

Technology has made our lives so much better. It's remarkable how easy and fast communication is today. The world truly is available on that little device we all hold in our hands. However, the question about technology that great leaders must ask is, "Am *I* in control or are my devices in control?"

There has been a ton written in recent years about how to increase personal productivity by more effectively managing your day. A quick search of books on Amazon using the phrase "morning routine" generates hundreds of titles. One thing most of these books have in common is recommending some sort of system to shut off the noise as you begin your day. It's about taking control of your time rather than allowing emails or text messages or phone calls to dictate where your attention goes.

I have routinely told the people who have worked as my assistants throughout the years that I don't answer my office phone. I've told them I'd prefer they don't answer it either – unless it's from a very small number of people on a list we created. The reason I work this way is that I have very specific things I want and need to get done during the day and I need to focus.

It has also been my routine to close my office door for periods of the time during each day. My assistants have acted as my bouncers to keep people from knocking on the door or interrupting me when the door is closed. I'm sure that sounds harsh to some of you, but I have found it to be a very effective approach to getting meaningful work done.

I also do not quickly respond to most emails. I refuse to live in an email app. I've tried that approach and I never got anything done. As soon as I started doing a task motivated by one email, my computer would ping with another email that interrupted what I was doing. Then as soon as I remembered what I was attempting to do before the new email distracted me, another one would pop into my inbox. It was enough to drive me insane.

I now check my email only a few times a day. I look for urgent messages and respond to them. I spend very little time reading emails I am copied on. I can't stand the cc line on emails. People feel like they need to copy every single person in an entire organization who might possibly have any interest or connection to the topic of that email. In the process, they decrease the productivity of far too many people.

I was in Singapore recently with a medical device manufacturing company. One of the executives told me she gets more than 2,000 emails a day. The number was staggering. She said that whenever she takes a week of vacation or holiday from work, she generally takes one additional day off just to respond to the emails she misses while gone. *She takes a vacation day just to respond to emails!* I was amazed at the commitment to her job – no one in America would ever take a vacation day to respond to work emails. Yet at the same time, I felt bad she had developed the habit of enabling 2,000 emails every day. How does she ever get anything done?

I know some people are paid to respond to emails. My team of assistants is paid to have their email and messaging apps open all day and to react to messages very quickly. Sales reps and customer service agents are expected to be available at a moment's notice as well.

But leaders are different. They are responsible for keeping others on course – for leading a team somewhere specific, and on time. Too frequently, they fail at Question #2: *Can You See & Describe the Destination?* because they are obsessed with today. If you can't turn off the incredibly loud noise that surrounds all of us in this Information Age, then you'll struggle mightily to be a great leader.

The best practice I see in this area is having a habit of turning off the noise daily *and* turning off the noise monthly or quarterly. How much time you need in silence each day depends on the industry you work in, the type of job you have, the issues you're confronting at the moment, and many other things. For some of us, we simply need 30-90 minutes a day free from distraction to make sure we're tackling the issues that are most important today – to help our organization hit its annual Key Results.

The monthly or quarterly escape from the noise should be done individually and with the help of your leadership team. That time should be focused on the Long-Range Target as well as the Annual Key Results. It is about the bigger picture.

The key to Question #8 is making sure you're managing your schedule and that your schedule isn't managing you. When your schedule is driven solely by which emails pop in or the fire of the hour, you tend to be very busy but not very productive.

ACTION ITEMS

- Ponder questions #5 – #8:

  - Are you willing to be a servant leader?

  - Are you allergic to the status quo?

  - Are you willing to change?

  - Are you able to shut off the noise?

- Consider an opportunity in the coming week where you could intentionally demonstrate your desire to serve those you lead. Put it on your calendar or enter in your "to-do" app. Make it a weekly priority. Then increase the frequency.

- Ask members of your team or peers if there is an area where you or the team are stuck doing it the way it's always been done. Get honest and candid feedback on the beliefs others hold about your support of innovation and new ideas. All of us can improve no matter how well we're doing in no matter how well we're doing in this area.

- Intentionally communicate, on a regular basis, changes you are making due to the feedback you're receiving. Being willing to change is different than actually demonstrating change.

- Schedule time away from distractions – particularly email and phone calls – on a daily, monthly, and quarterly basis. There are many tools available to help manage digital distractions. Consider utilizing just one of them over the next week.

Conclusion:
Final Thoughts

*t*he Executive Vice President (EVP) I mentioned earlier in this book came back to Phoenix every quarter or so. He was the person who made sure I knew my future hinged on the success of the radio station turnaround project I've discussed throughout this book. The meeting I attended with him – about six months after that striking moment on the way back to his hotel (see Chapter 4) – will always stand out in my mind. It's a fitting conclusion to our story about leadership.

The turnaround project was a smashing success. The ratings and revenue of the radio station skyrocketed. After a tremendous amount of blood, sweat, and tears (well, maybe not blood but plenty of sweat and tears), by an incredibly talented and committed team, the station returned to greatness. I am proud that the station not only got back on track but that it has sustained successful results for almost a decade now.

Shortly after the metrics hit and exceeded the company's targets, I found myself facing the EVP again. There were 15-20 people in the room, seated at tables set up in a U-shape. This meeting was the first one I attended where I was no longer the guy who was carrying around the stress of an uncertain turnaround project. I came to the meeting as the leader of a team that had now successfully pulled off a remarkable accomplishment.

I walked in feeling excited. No longer would I have to defend our plan. No longer would I have to answer questions about whether I knew what I was doing. No longer would I have to fight for more time or justify anything. Instead, I anticipated the EVP would start the quarterly strategy session acknowledging and celebrating the incredible accomplishment of my team.

It didn't happen.

The meeting started the same as it always did. There was no celebration. There was no applause. There was no gratitude. About 20-30 minutes into the meeting, as the group was deep into a discussion about the issues of the moment, the EVP made a side comment. It was something like, "We know Russ's plan worked. Now what we need to do is…"

I actually laughed out loud. I couldn't hold it back. In the middle of that serious dialogue, my mouth opened and several chuckles came out. Everyone turned and looked at me. They were confused about why I was laughing. Someone smiled and asked, "Russ, what are you laughing about?" I apologized, said I had thought of something unrelated, and excused my interruption. The meeting carried on.

A short time later, the group took a ten-minute break. My boss and I passed each other in the hallway leading to the bathroom. He pulled me aside and said he thought he knew why I had laughed out loud.

I said, "I guess that was the reward wasn't it?"

"What do you mean?" he asked.

"I guess when ___ (the EVP) made that side comment about how 'We know Russ's plan worked,' that was my acknowledgment from him my team pulled off the turnaround."

My boss responded, "Yeah, I think that's about all you're going to get from him."

Being a leader is hard. Leading that turnaround brought with it so many sleepless nights. It tested me and stretched me. There were times I wish I hadn't decided to lead that project at all. But I stuck with it and gave it everything I had.

In the end, the real reward was incredibly sweet. It obviously didn't come from that Executive Vice President. Yes, I received the healthy bonus payments I had negotiated as part of my monetary compensation for successfully leading that project. But the real reward came in how the experience affected me. It came in all the lessons I learned. It came in watching others overcome challenges and experience greater success than they had ever previously achieved. It came in the story we – the members of that team and I – wrote together. The reward came in the increased capacity it created in me to guide others.

Deciding to lead that project changed me in wonderful ways. Leadership is an amazing thing. Is leading a team worth all you go through as the leader? The answer to that question often depends on the day you ask it. But in the end, the answer is *yes*. It is very much worth it.

Part of what I deeply enjoy about what I do for a living is watching teams that are seemingly stuck suddenly start achieving results that once felt out of reach. The shift is always due to leaders who change the culture of their teams by demonstrating the principles we've discussed in this brief book.

Organizations get stuck when leaders are stuck.

It comes down to accountability. Too many people charged with leading teams externalize the need for change as they seek to transform the teams they work with. They blame members of the team, certain departments in their organization, someone above them on the org chart, the economy, or the customer for the problems they're having achieving results. What I've tried to do in this book is to help all of us – anyone who has made a decision to lead – realize we need to look inward before we look outward.

Most of us have been elevated to positions of additional responsibility because of the impact we had as an individual contributor. And yet when we were given a fancier role, title, or office, most of us were given little to no training on how to become a great leader.

Often when I am standing on a stage somewhere in the world speaking to a group of leaders, I am surprised by the amount of applause that fills the room at the conclusion of our time together. At first, I thought this was a reflection of my skills or ability. I have come to realize it is actually an indication of just how much leaders want and need *any* assistance to become stronger leaders.

I started this book by asking you to visualize the two of us sitting down together for lunch or in a coffee shop having a conversation. I hope the questions I've asked have helped you reflect on how you're leading others.

This book, like every book on leadership, doesn't contain all the answers. It's intended primarily to get you to think about yourself in a new way and focus on a few key areas where you might put in a little more effort.

This is my first book – and I'm told by my friends that have written New York Times bestsellers that the first is always the worst. Thank you for your patience in reading my worst book ever! If you found some value in it, I'd greatly appreciate it if you'd leave a review on Amazon or even better tell a friend or two about it. If you hated this book, I hope your Wi-Fi just went down and that you'll experience short-term memory loss.

As someone who has decided to lead, I hope you will make – or have made – the same decision.

At the beginning of this book, I shared with you that I sat down to write it in an effort to help build more great leaders. This is only one part of those efforts. As I've mentioned on previous pages, I have created an online course that goes into much greater depth on each of these topics and provides coaching on how to incorporate the lessons here into your life. My desire is to expand your influence, help you achieve your purpose, improve your lifestyle, and teach you how to get others to do the things you need them to do to accelerate achievement of results.

You can sign up for the online course as well as join a private Facebook Group where I go live every month to share trends I'm seeing, provide additional conversation topics and answer your questions.

All of these tools and resources can be accessed at *decidetoleadbook.com.* If you've already signed up for the course or Facebook Group, I'm thrilled that you've now finished this book and congratulate you on the time and money you're investing in improving your leadership skills. The investment will pay off as your ability to get others to produce even greater results improves. And it will.

Thank you for the time you've spent considering my ideas.

I can't wait to learn from you in the private Decide to Lead Facebook Group and the course at *decidetoleadbook.com!*

The Decide to Lead Questions

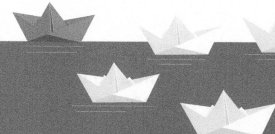

1 Do You Want to be a Leader?

2 Can You See and Desribe the Destination?

3 Can You Delegate to & Develop Others?

4 Are You Willing to Stand Alone?

Ways to Strengthen Your Leadership Skills Right Now

THE DECIDE TO LEAD ONLINE COURSE

If you haven't signed up already for the FREE Decide to Lead online course – what are you waiting for? Russ takes the concepts in this book and teaches them on screen in virtual training.

You can begin taking the course on your phone, laptop, or tablet in the next five minutes by simply going to decidetoleadbook. com and signing up.

Here's what you'll get:

- Video recordings of Russ teaching the models and tools in this book

- Worksheet pages that you can fill out while taking the course that move the concepts in this book from good ideas to actionable steps you can take in your life to begin seeing impact immediately

- Additional stories, models, and tools that Russ didn't want to squeeze into this book but that he teaches leaders of the companies he consults and shares for the first time publically in the course

- Free access to the private Facebook Group where Russ goes live at least once a month to answer questions and share additional insights and trends

- Case studies from Amazon, Chick-fil-A, and other organizations where leaders are achieving incredible results

The course is FREE! Russ is offering it as additional learning available to those who have purchased the book. You can learn more about the course or sign up right now at *decidetoleadbook. com*

THE PRIVATE FACEBOOK GROUP

Along with the course Russ is offering access to his private Facebook Group for leaders. Here's what you'll find inside the FREE Facebook Group:

- Private live broadcasts with Russ every month where he teaches on camera in front of a flipchart and shares trends he's seeing and new learnings.

- Private access during those group live broadcasts to ask Russ questions and get him to respond to your particular leadership challenge or situation.

- Access to collaborate with leaders in similar situations to yours. You can post a question, share ideas, and learn from people trying to become more effective leaders.

- First access to Russ's future courses, books, and events. You'll be alerted to these things before the general public and offered a discounted rate as a member of the private Facebook Group.

- To join the private Facebook Group go to *decidetoleadbook. com* for the link and instructions.

LEADERSHIP COACHING & CONSULTING SERVICES

Russ takes on a limited number of coaching and consulting clients each year. He offers monthly coaching and consulting with individual leaders or leadership teams. These sessions are typically done virtually over Zoom, on-site, or over the phone.

To learn more about Russ's coaching and consulting services please reach out to the consulting team at *coaching@decidetoleadbook.com* or find more information at *decidetoleadbook.com*

About the Author

Russ Hill

Russ Hill is a leadership coach, consultant, author, and host of The Culture Hacks Podcast. Each year he speaks to and consults tens of thousands of leaders across the world.

The organizations Russ works with include three of the Fortune 10 companies (the ten largest companies in the United States based on revenue) as well as dozens of other organizations ranging from national restaurant chains to healthcare companies to defense contractors and car manufacturers.

Russ offers online courses, live webinars, and group coaching services for team leaders, executives, and entrepreneurs.

Russ is active on social media including LinkedIn, Facebook, Instagram, and YouTube.

You can connect with him at any of the social media platforms listed here:

Instagram: @russleads

Twitter: @russleads

LinkedIn: www.linkedin.com/in/russleads

Facebook: www.facebook.com/groups/culturechampion

Apple Podcasts/Spotify:
search "Culture Hacks with Russ Hill"

decidetoleadbook.com